Christine Holland and Stephen Grocott helped in the preparation of this book. We would like to thank the many people in Garston who supplied us with fascinating information about their town.

Schenk, Christopher
    Jubilee terrace. – (Beans).
    1. Garston, Eng. – Streets – Juvenile literature
    2. Garston, Eng. – Social life and customs – Juvenile literature
    I. Title II. Series
    942.7'53   DA690.G24/

ISBN 0-7136-1975-9

Acknowledgments

All the photographs are by Jeremy Finlay except for the following:

Mrs Edwards 24a, 25a, 25b; Ernie Fletcher 13a; Valerie Haines 10a; Liverpool Central Library 17, 22, 23b; Liverpool City Engineer's Department 15; Frances Mackay 6a, 6b; Mary Evans Picture Library 12a, 16a; Museum of English Rural Life 9c; Radio Times Hulton Picture Library 2b, 5b, 7, 8a, 8b, 10b, 11, 16b, 23a, 24b; Christopher Schenk 10a, 13a, 24a, 25a, 25b; Whitworth Art Gallery endpapers, 21.

A & C Black (Publishers) Limited
35 Bedford Row, London WC1R 4JH
ISBN 0 7136 1975 9

© Christopher Schenk and Jeremy Finlay 1979

All rights reserved. No part of this publication may be reproduced, stored in a retrieval system, or transmitted, in any form or by any means, electronic, mechanical, photocopying, recording or otherwise, without the prior permission of A & C Black (Publishers) Limited

Printed in Great Britain by
Hazell, Watson & Viney, Aylesbury, Bucks

Jubilee Terrace

Christopher Schenk
Photographs by Jeremy Finlay

Adam & Charles Black · London

Jubilee Terrace has been standing for quite a long time. Like every street, it has a story to tell. Children have been born here. They have played in the street. They have grown up and gone out to work. They have got married and had children of their own.

There are all sorts of clues that can help you find out the story of the street. One clue is the name 'Jubilee Terrace'. It couldn't have been Queen Elizabeth's Silver Jubilee. The houses look too old for that.

In the next street there is a date – 1889. Queen Victoria had Jubilees in 1887 and 1897. Jubilee Terrace must have been built round about then. This means that the houses are nearly one hundred years old.

People used to live very differently in those days. There are lots of ways of finding out how they used to live.

One of the best ways is to ask old people. They often like to talk about how they used to live when they were young.

There are many old people who have lived in Jubilee Terrace all their lives. In fact they were born there. In those days women didn't usually go to hospital to have babies. Their babies were born at home.

Queen Victoria

The houses in Jubilee Terrace are quite small. They've got three bedrooms. In the old days many people had large families. It was quite common to have seven children and there was even one family with seventeen.

It must have been quite a squash for a big family to live in one of these houses. There wasn't room for everyone to have a bed. Usually the mother and father would sleep in one bedroom. Another would have all the girls sleeping together in one bed. The boys would share a bed in the third bedroom.

One man had such a big family that there wasn't any room for him to sleep in his own house. He had to get a job working nights, so that he could have a bed to sleep in during the day.

Of course with so many people living in a small space, there was a lot of housework. There was lots of cooking to do, and washing up. There were many clothes to wash and iron, and it was a hard job to keep the house clean and tidy. The children were given jobs to help with the housework.

For instance one of the older girls would empty the ashes out of the grate every morning. The younger children ran errands when they came home from school.

When these old people were young, there wasn't any electricity in Jubilee Terrace. There are still gas lamps in one of the houses. All the houses used to have gas lamps just like these. You can't just press a switch and get some light. You have to open a gas tap and then strike a match and light the lamp carefully, making sure you don't break the mantle.

There were gas lamps in the street as well. Every night, when it got dark, a man had to come round with a light on the end of a long pole so that he could reach up to light the street lamps.

The boys and girls took it in turns to have baths. One night all the girls had to go to bed early. The tub was filled with hot water from the boiler. One of the boys got in and was scrubbed clean. While he dried, one of his brothers got into the same water. It took too long to heat water for everyone to have a clean tubful.

Next night it would be the girls' turn and the boys would have to go to bed early.

There was only one tap in the sink – a cold one. If you wanted hot water you had to heat it in a boiler. This took quite a long time over a coal fire.

The bath didn't have any taps at all. It was just a tin tub that you could hang up in the kitchen until it was needed. There wasn't a bathroom either. If you wanted to go to the toilet you had to go outside, and you had your bath in the back kitchen.

Monday was washing day. With a big family there was always a lot of washing to be done.

These days you can put your washing into an automatic washing-machine with some soap powder, and the machine does all the work.

In the old days, everything had to be done by hand. There wasn't even any washing powder. You had to get a block of soap and shave off bits with a knife.

Using a dolly peg

Airing clothes on a clothes rack

The water had to be heated up in the boiler to begin with. Then the clothes were put into the tin tub. They were joggled about in the soapy water with a wooden thing called a dolly peg. It was hard work, pushing the clothes around until they got really clean.

Usually they were washed twice in hot water and then rinsed twice in cold water. A little bit of 'dolly blue' was added to the shirts and the linen to get them really white. Then they were soaked in starch and water so that they would look crisp and smart when they were dried and ironed.

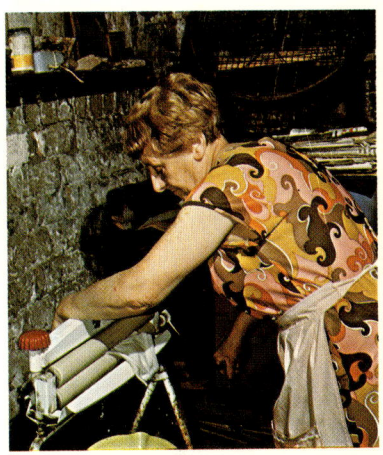

To get the water out you had to squeeze the clothes through a mangle. That was hard work too.

When they were nearly dry, the clothes were ironed – not with an electric iron of course. You had to use a flat iron that was warmed by the fire. You could only iron a little bit at a time because the iron cooled down and had to go back by the fire to warm up again. You could tell when it was hot enough by spitting on it. The spit would sizzle when it was hot. The iron was very heavy because it was made of solid iron.

A flat iron resting on its stand

The clothes were aired on a clothes rack let down by pulleys in front of the fire.

The corner shop

A 'wait and see' pie

People didn't have electric cookers either and many people didn't even have a gas ring. They did all their cooking by the coal fire.

Just by the fire there was a metal stand called a hob. You could swing this over towards the heat and put a saucepan or a kettle on it. In fact there was usually a kettle whistling away on the hob.

The ovens, next to the fire, were used for all the baking. They were very good for making bread. You could leave the dough to rise in the top oven and then bake in the bottom oven which was hotter.

In the summer there wasn't always a fire, so the children were sent to the baker's with the bread dough in a pillow case. He would bake it in his oven for a penny.

On Sunday you could buy your dinner from the corner shop. You could have rabbit, potatoes, carrots, turnips and onions, all for a few pennies.

During the week the food wasn't so good. Sometimes they had 'rattle in the pan'. This was potatoes, bacon and onions fried up in a frying pan with a bit of water. There was never enough of it so it used to rattle.

When there was anything left over, it was put into a 'see pie' – that meant 'wait and see' pie. You never knew what was going to be underneath the pastry.

There weren't many sweets for the children to buy, but a special favourite was cinder toffee. It was just like the inside of a 'Crunchie' bar.

Instead of sweets they often bought carrots, or cut fruit. If an apple or a pear was bruised, the shopkeeper would sell it cheaply to the children.

They also liked to buy cherries because then they could play a game with the cherry stones. It was called 'cherry wags'. You threw your cherry stones up a drainpipe and if they hit someone else's stones on the way down, you could keep them. It was a bit like marbles.

They played a lot of games in the street. It was quite safe because there was hardly any traffic – just a horse-drawn milk cart or a shopkeeper's barrow.

But there was a park nearby for them to play in too. It's still there and you can see from the pictures that it hasn't changed much. But the children look quite different.

In the old days there was a park keeper. One of his jobs was to keep the boys out of the girls' playground. They weren't supposed to play together.

Just up the road from Jubilee Terrace is a school which was built round about the same time. There are now almost three hundred children in the school, but there used to be more than a thousand. It must have been difficult to fit them all in.

Children went to school at the age of three and stayed in the same school until they were fourteen.

Every school has a log book. The head teacher writes down important things that happen in the school. The school near Jubilee Terrace has some old log books that tell us a lot about the past.

> Jany 16th: Absent from School between 10.45 & 1.30 to visit Education Office Lpool. in regard to Mr Jones & the Salary he is claiming.
> Very cold to day - Easterly wind -
> Absentee notes state reason of being away is "No boots" in majority of cases - no coats in others

An entry from the school log book

For instance, some of the children couldn't come to school in the winter because they had no boots. Other children couldn't come because they had no coats. They would have needed their coats – the only heating was an open fire. The children sitting at the back got very cold.

It's not surprising that many children became ill. Because the school was so crowded, germs spread easily. Sometimes the whole school had to be closed because nearly all the children were ill. Once, schools all over the city had to be closed because so many children had 'flu.

There wasn't enough paper for everyone to write on, so the younger children wrote with their fingers in sand trays. Older children used slates that could be wiped clean.

One of the exciting things that happened was a visit from the king. The school log book says that nearly 100 boys went off to the local football ground to greet King George V.

16 King George V visits Garston

> to see their Majesties.
>
> 11th: Twenty boys who had been specially selected to take part in the "living Union Jack" and nearly 100 boys, assembled in the afternoon & proceeded to the ground – prior to which they each received a packet of cakes & sweets

We can find out a bit more about this event from the local newspaper. At the football ground the boys from schools all over the city were dressed in red, white or blue. They stood on the football pitch to form a living flag: a Union Jack to welcome the king.

The old bobbin factory

One of the women who used to work at the bobbin factory

Nearly everybody left school at the age of fourteen when they started work.

You can find out what jobs people did by looking in a street directory. Most large towns and cities have directories in the public library.

...son secretary		Lord
...ge Henry caretaker	1	Stansfield Willie foremn. bobbin se
...td. dispensing chemists	3	Hey Sam bobbin turner
...ohn H. & Son cabinet	5	Duckworth Mrs. Margaret Ann
	7	Crabtree John
Indigent Blind	9	Collins John
...ittlewood supt	11	Burrell John W. brakesman
Littlewood matron	13	Gaskill Thomas stoker
...rch for the Blind	15	Norman James bobbin maker
Hope st	17	Fisher William joiner
	19	Madden John labourer
K SQUARE—E	21	Cunningham Robert labourer
Hardwick st	23	Birkenhead Mrs. Emma
Margaret shopkeeper	25	Smith John labourer
...hristine	27	Terry Edward book keeper
	29	Robinson Albert fitter
Joseph butcher	31	Allwood John labourer
...n labourer	33	Woollett Charles Howard barma
...vatchman	35	Salt Leonard template worker
...arriet	37	Burgess Adam labourer
french polisher	39	Henderson John copper worker
	43	Fillingham Frank tinsmith
...llen	2	Barker Fielden mechanic
butcher	4	Harris Richard Henry warehouse
	6	Almond Robert steam raiser
warehouseman	8	Salt James
	10	Stansfield Wilfred
CK ST.—E	12	Brown William iron roofer
Prescot st	14	Newton Arthur gas maker
...in carter	16	Walsh Mrs. Ann
...abourer	18	Young Alexander bobbin turner
Isabella shopkeeper	20	Lambert Thomas George laboure
Hardwick square	22	Gibson Joshua Henry painter
...atrick clerk	24	Hodgson John
Jude's place North	26	Coulthard Robert wood turner
...rch	28	Calder David boiler maker
Jude's place South	30	Williams Lewis joiner
...zabeth	32	Williams Robert Henry copper wo
...k	36	Stanton Alfred
	38	Barrow Ernest marine mechanic

A lot of the people who lived in Jubilee Terrace made bobbins. That's because there was a bobbin works at the end of the road. It's still there now but it doesn't make bobbins any longer.

A bobbin is made of wood. Cotton is wound onto it. These bobbins were sent out to India where they were used in cotton factories.

Some of the old people have still got bobbins that they made.

When they first started working in the bobbin factory as children, they didn't get paid much. They gave all their wages to their parents and had just a bit of pocket money in return.

If they came to work on time every day and they were always clean, they got a certificate at the end of the year. They were also given an extra week's wages.

But it was quite difficult to get to work on time every day. They had to be there by six o'clock in the morning.

There used to be a man called Enoch Elliott, who was called the knocker-upper. He went round with a long bamboo pole with wires on the end of it. He would stand in the street and tap on the bedroom windows with the wires, when it was time for people to get up.

Later on, the bobbin factory got a siren which went off at half-past five and woke you up, whether you worked there or not. Nobody minded the siren. They used it as an alarm clock because most people got up early anyway. There was an extra buzzer at five to six to warn people they might be late. When that buzzer went you could see all the slowcoaches hurrying along.

They worked until eight o'clock in the morning and then went home for breakfast. They had another break for dinner and after that they didn't stop work until five o'clock in the evening.

Jubilee Terrace is now in the middle of a large city with nothing but streets for miles around.

But some of the old people can remember when there were fields close by. There was a stream and a little wood just the other side of the school where the children used to go and pick bluebells. The woods were private and they weren't supposed to play in them. Sometimes they were chased away by a gamekeeper with a dog.

There was a farm nearby. All the milk came from the farm. The milkman didn't deliver milk in bottles then. Instead he came round with a cart drawn by a horse. He had a big milk churn on the back. People came out of their houses with their jugs and he ladled milk out of the churn for them.

To get to the city centre you had to pass through the countryside. There were horse-drawn omnibuses that left every hour. They had open tops which must have been nice on a sunny day, but rather cold in winter.

There were also trams. These had open tops too, and ran on rails just like a train. At first they were pulled by horses but later on they were powered by electricity.

At the end of Jubilee Terrace there was a herb shop. Friends would go there together for a soft drink made from herbs. There was sasaparilla or dandelion and burdock.

In the evenings there weren't any televisions to watch. Sometimes people would go by tram to a picture house or a dance hall, but often they walked around the streets, meeting their friends and talking.

Queuing at the cinema (picture house)

When King George V had his Silver Jubilee, there was a street party in the Terrace. Many of the families also went on an outing in a charabanc to see the king. A charabanc is an old-fashioned coach.

The people of Jubilee Terrace still get together on special occasions. For Queen Elizabeth's Silver Jubilee they had another street party and everyone joined in the fun.

The 1935 Silver Jubilee party ▶

▲ The 1953 coronation party for Queen Elizabeth II

So now Queen Elizabeth's Jubilee has become part of the history of Jubilee Terrace – a history that's still going on...

25